TRACKING DOWN
THE
VICTORIANS
IN BRITAIN

TRACKING DOWN

THE VICTORIANS

IN BRITAIN

LIZ GOGERLY

W
FRANKLIN WATTS
LONDON · SYDNEY

This edition published in 2013 by Franklin Watts

Copyright © 2013 Franklin Watts

Franklin Watts
338 Euston Road
London NW1 3BH

Franklin Watts Australia
Level 17/207 Kent Street
Sydney, NSW 2000

A CIP catalogue record for this book is available
from the British Library.

Dewey number: 941'.081

ISBN 978 1 4451 1659 4

Printed in China

Franklin Watts is a division of Hachette Children's Books,
an Hachette UK company.

www.hachette.co.uk

Editor: Sarah Ridley
Design: John Christopher/White Design
Editor in Chief: John C. Miles
Art director: Jonathan Hair

Picture credits:
Abbey-Cwm-Hir: 22b. Artmedia/HIP/Topfoto: 7. Barnes/Topfoto: 20t.
Connie G Barwick.About.com Cross Stitch: 22t. Blists Hill Victorian Town/The Ironbridge Gorge Museum Trust: 21.
City of London/HIP/Topfoto: 14b. Ian Dagnall/Alamy: 10. Mary Evans PL: 8, 18b, 19. Gladstone Pottery Museum,
Stoke-on-Trent : 27b. The Granger Collection/Topfoto: 14t, 16t, 29t.Great Cressingham Victorian School: 25. Jeff
Greenberg/Image Works/Topfoto: 20b. Judges Lodgings, Presteigne, Wales: 29b. Nadia MacKenzie/National Trust PL:
23tr. NRM/Pictorial Collection/Science & Society PL: 18t. Old Operating Theatre, London: 27t. James
Osmond/Alamy: front cover, 16b. Doug Pearson/Jon Arnold Images/Alamy: 11b. Picturepoint/Topham: 24, 28. Pixel
Youth Movement 3/Alamy: 15. Jon Prior Images/Alamy: 12. Courtesy of Queen Street Mill Textile Museum, Burnley:
13t. Mark Sutherland/National Trust PL: 23bl. Topfoto: 26. UK City Images/Topfoto: 17t. Courtesy of the
Verdant Works, Dundee: 13b. Woodmansterne/Topfoto: 9t, 9b. Adam Woolfitt/Robert Harding PL/Alamy: 11c.
World History Archive/Topfoto: 6.   *Every attempt has been made to clear copyright. Should there be any inadvertent
omission please apply to the publisher for rectification.*

CONTENTS

WHO WERE THE VICTORIANS?

In 1837, Princess Victoria became queen at the age of 18. As Queen Victoria she ruled the country until her death in 1901. That period of time is known as the Victorian period and the people who lived during that period are called the Victorians.

Great changes

The Victorians lived through a time of great change. Britain was at the heart of the Industrial Revolution and was nicknamed 'the workshop of the world'. Mass production of everything from clothes and food to bicycles and household equipment meant better lives for nearly everyone. New inventions, such as the electric light bulb, the telephone and the camera, changed everyday life.

By 1850, Britain was the most powerful industrial nation in the world. Queen Victoria's husband, Prince Albert, was fascinated by industry and new technology. In 1851, he helped to organise the Great Exhibition to show off the inventions of the time. The exhibition, held at London's Hyde Park, brought together products from all over the world. To many people it was the symbol of the Victorian age.

← Queen Victoria in her coronation robes, 1838.

↑ A view of part of the Great Exhibition, held in London in 1851.

GO VISIT

Local Museums and Galleries

A good place to start learning more about the Victorians is local museums and art galleries. Many were built in Victorian times for the enjoyment of ordinary working people to help them learn more about art and culture. Wolverhampton Art Gallery opened in 1884 and Blackburn Museum and Art Gallery opened in 1874. Both are good examples of museums built in Victorian times that are still open to the public.

The Victorian legacy

Evidence of what the Victorians built is all around us in our towns and cities. Look up and you may see Victorian street lamps. Look down and the pavements you're walking on may have been laid in Victorian times. And, if you could look underground there may even be sewers that were built by the Victorians. Many people live in homes of all sizes built by Victorian builders. Large villas and mansions, which were built as homes for rich industrialists, still survive as schools, nursing homes or flats. Many of our public parks were created by the Victorians to give working people some contact with nature. Perhaps you can track down the Victorian railway stations, town halls, hospitals, schools and other public buildings in your local area.

Queen Victoria and Prince Albert had grand royal palaces. However, it was at their country houses on the Isle of Wight and in the Scottish Highlands that they really felt at home.

The Royal homes

Queen Victoria was born at Kensington Palace on 24 May 1819. In 1837, she became the first British monarch to make Buckingham Palace the main royal residence. Other royal palaces were Windsor Castle in Berkshire and the Royal Pavilion at Brighton. In 1839, Queen Victoria proposed marriage to her German cousin Prince Albert of Saxe-Coburg and Gotha. They were married in 1840 and proved a great love match. Over the next 18 years they had nine children together and became the model of the perfect family to many Victorians.

⬇ When Prince Albert died in 1861 Queen Victoria spent much of her time at Osborne House (next page) and Balmoral Castle (below, shown in a painting of 1880).

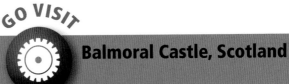

GO VISIT

Balmoral Castle, Scotland

Victoria and Albert had a holiday home at Balmoral in Scotland. Prince Albert bought the Balmoral Estate for Victoria in 1852. The castle was completed in 1856 and Victoria called it her "dear paradise". Balmoral Castle is still used by the royal family but, for a few months each year, the public can visit parts of the castle and its gardens.

Osborne House

Victoria liked Buckingham Palace but, with a growing family, the young royals began looking for a home away from court life in London. The Queen wanted, "... a place of one's own, quiet and retired". In 1845, they bought the Osborne Estate near Cowes on the Isle of Wight and started building their new home. Family life was important to the royals and they had the children's nursery built over their own private apartments. The house had the latest fittings, such as showers, and later on electric lighting and telephones were added. There was also a billiard room where Victoria learned to play the game.

GO VISIT

Osborne House and the Swiss Cottage

Victoria wanted a family home that was richly decorated but comfortable and welcoming. You can decide if she achieved this by visiting Osborne House yourself. One of the highlights of a visit is the Swiss Cottage. It was a birthday present to the royal children in 1854.

⬆ The Swiss Cottage at Osborne House had a garden where the royal children grew their own vegetables.

⬇ Osborne House was built in an Italian style.

Victorian Britain was a constitutional monarchy. This meant that Queen Victoria was head of state but parliament ran the country. The Houses of Parliament, where government sits today, were built in Victorian times.

Government

Victoria was only 18 when she became queen, but she was interested in politics. She had daily meetings with the prime minister, Lord Melbourne. They became good friends and he taught her how British government was run. Although she did not have much political power, her support was important to all of the prime ministers who took power during her long reign. All the important decisions were made by Parliament but much more power was given to local government during the Victorian period. Based at the new town halls, local government focused on health, housing and law and order.

⬇ Manchester Town Hall was completed in 1887.

GO VISIT

Victorian Town Halls

Manchester Town Hall is one of many Victorian buildings built in the same Gothic style as the Houses of Parliament. This striking building has a main clock tower and at the front there is a memorial to Prince Albert. Perhaps you can discover when your local town hall was built. If it is a Victorian building, does it have the same Gothic design as Manchester Town Hall and the Houses of Parliament?

The Houses of Parliament

One of the most famous landmarks in London is the Houses of Parliament, also known as the Palace of Westminster. The grand Gothic building on the north bank of the River Thames was started in 1840 and took 30 years to build. It replaced the original Westminster Palace which burned down in 1834. The new building was the work of architects Sir Charles Barry and Augustus Pugin. The palace has several towers including the Clock Tower which houses the bell Big Ben. The tallest is Victoria Tower, named after the Queen, which reaches 98.5 metres high.

Inside there are over 1,100 rooms and 100 staircases arranged over four floors. The richly decorated House of Lords has beautiful stained glass windows. You can take a tour of the Houses of Parliament but tickets must be arranged through your local Member of Parliament (MP). Any visitor over the age of eleven can climb up the 334 spiralling stone steps leading to Big Ben in the Clock Tower.

⬧ A view of the Houses of Parliament, Big Ben and Westminster Bridge.

⬧ Inside the House of Lords. The House of Lords has red benches and the House of Commons has green benches.

The invention of steam power helped to turn Britain into the most powerful industrial nation in the world.

Steam engines

In early Victorian times, steam engines were being used to power machinery. They were used in factories, mines and mills, and later on farms. Steam engines were not a new invention but the Victorians designed new and improved engines. As a result Britain led the way in iron and steel production. Its manufacturing industry became the envy of the world. At the Great Exhibition of 1851 (see page 6), most of the machinery and new inventions were made in Britain.

▼ The steam-powered traction engine provided the power to do many of the jobs on farms in the late-19th century.

↑ A steam engine on the ground floor of a mill was capable of running hundreds of machines at one time, as shown here at Queen Street Mill.

Queen Street Mill

Steam also powered the power looms used to weave cotton cloth. By the time Queen Victoria took the throne, over half of all British exports were cotton textiles. In 1850, there were over 250,000 power looms in Britain and 177,000 of these were in Lancashire. Queen Street Mill in Burnley, Lancashire is the last remaining mill in Europe where you can still see steam-powered looms in action. You can experience the noise that the mill workers had to endure every day.

GO VISIT

Verdant Works, Dundee

Dundee in Scotland became the centre of Britain's jute industry in Victorian times. Jute is a natural fibre which can be woven into hessian cloth or made into rope. The Verdant Works in Dundee were opened as a jute mill in 1833. Today, it is a living museum where you can see working looms and hear stories about the workers.

← Visitors to Verdant Works, dressed in period costume.

THE RAILWAY AGE

At the beginning of Victoria's reign, the main form of transport was the horse. Queen Victoria became the first British monarch to travel by train.

A better way to travel

Horses were a slow and expensive way of transporting people and goods. Scientists and inventors scrambled to invent bigger and better steam locomotives to do the job of horses. The breakthrough came in 1830, when George and Robert Stephenson created a steam engine called *Rocket*. It was faster and more efficient than anything that had gone before, travelling at speeds of over 48 kilometres per hour. It ran on the Liverpool and Manchester Railway line and was an inspiration for railway owners.

▲ Railway workers prepare George and Robert Stephenson's *Rocket* for a journey while spectators look on.

Royal railway

"What a curious thing!" said Queen Victoria in 1837, when she saw her first steam train. Like many other Victorians she viewed this new invention with suspicion. Compared to horses, trains seemed fast, dangerous and dirty. In June 1841, Victoria made her first journey by rail in her brand new state carriage and was "quite charmed by it".

◄ This Victorian engraving shows Victoria and Albert relaxing in the royal saloon train carriage.

↑ Inside the National
Railway Museum, York.

Railway mania

Victoria's love of the train helped to
make railways popular with everyone.
Throughout the late 1830s and the
1840s, money was poured into
developing Britain's new railway
network. In 1845, 3,928 kilometres of
railway had been built. By 1900, there
were over 30,062 kilometres of track.
In that time the railway had
transformed people's lives. Millions of
ordinary people used the train to get to
work or go on holiday. The trains
carried everything from raw materials
and heavy goods to fresh food, daily
papers and the mail.

GO VISIT

**National Railway Museum,
York**

You can track the history of the
railway by visiting the National
Railway Museum in York. Visitors
can see the replica of Stephenson's
Rocket and many restored
Victorian steam engines. Also on
display is a carriage that Queen
Victoria travelled in herself. If you
can't visit the museum, take a
look at your local station. Many of
these were built by the Victorians
and are still in use today.

The British also led the way in engineering. One of the most daring and exciting engineers of the day was Isambard Kingdom Brunel.

Genius engineer

Isambard Kingdom Brunel was born in Portsmouth in 1806. Brunel was just 20 when he assisted his father, the engineer Sir Marc Isambard Brunel, in building a tunnel under the River Thames. In 1833, Brunel began work on the Great Western Railway which ran between London and Bristol. He designed the tracks, tunnels, bridges, viaducts and the stations along the route.

← A photograph of Isambard Kingdom Brunel standing in front of the huge chains used to launch his ship, the *Great Eastern*.

GO VISIT

Clifton Suspension Bridge, Bristol

Brunel is remembered for his bridges, especially the Clifton Suspension Bridge in Bristol – also the home of his steamship SS *Great Britain*. Brunel was just 24 when he won a competition to design the bridge. The project was daring because the bridge spanned 213 metres over the Avon Gorge. Lack of funds meant the bridge was not completed until 1864, five years after Brunel's death. At the time it was the longest bridge in the world.

The world's first ocean liner

In 1835, Brunel announced his plans to build a steamship that could cross the Atlantic to America. Brunel's idea was that passengers could buy a ticket at Paddington railway station which would take them all the way to New York. Many Victorian scientists did not believe a steamship could carry enough coal for the crossing. Brunel set to work designing and building a wooden ship that was big enough to hold enough coal. When it was launched in 1837, Brunel's steamship the *Great Western* was the largest ship in the world. It made its first successful voyage across the Atlantic in 1838. Brunel was triumphant and began work on his next steamship.

↑ The SS *Great Britain*, shown here in her dock at Bristol, travelled around the world 32 times.

↓ Brunel's Clifton Suspension Bridge is still in use today.

The SS *Great Britain*

The SS *Great Britain* was even bigger and is credited with being the forerunner of all modern ocean liners. The wrought iron hull was revolutionary and Brunel chose the newly-invented screw propeller to drive his boat. In 1845, the SS *Great Britain* made its first Atlantic crossing in a record-breaking 14 days. Today, the ship is moored in the dock where it was built in Bristol. Visitors can explore the restored ship and see the body of the ship, the engine rooms and the screw propeller. They can also see the tiny first-class passenger cabins and the dining room used by Victorian passengers.

BESIDE THE SEASIDE

Holidays to the seaside became popular with rich and poor Victorians. They enjoyed the sea air and the variety of entertainment on offer.

Steaming to the sea

The coming of the railways helped to develop many British seaside resorts. In the south of England places such as Brighton and Bournemouth became popular. In the days before train travel it took six hours to reach Brighton from London on horseback. By train the same journey took just two hours. To begin with rail fares were expensive but when fares were cut, ordinary working people were able to go to the seaside for the day. Blackpool on the north-west coast of England became popular with workers from nearby industrial areas. Meanwhile Scarborough on the north-east coast attracted a 'posher' more middle-class crowd of tourists. Llandudno and Rhyl offered Welsh workers a getaway. In Scotland many resorts grew along the Firth of Clyde and Firth of Forth because of the steamboats that travelled up and down the water.

▲ This Victorian poster advertises cheap fares to Cornwall.

GO VISIT

Blackpool Tower, Blackpool

One of the most striking Victorian tourist attractions on the north-west coast is Blackpool Tower. The tower was modelled on the Eiffel Tower in Paris and rises up 153 metres. It was opened in 1894 and you can still visit the Tower, Ballroom and Aquarium.

➤ A Victorian photograph showing tourists in Blackpool.

Pier spotting

If you live in a seaside town or you visit a place regularly, perhaps you could discover its history. Many seaside resorts that developed at this time still have Victorian railway stations, large hotels and smaller boarding houses. They also have piers, bandstands, pleasure gardens, aquariums and other Victorian tourist attractions.

Piers are one of the easiest structures to spot as they stretch out to sea from the land. Originally, they were built as places for steamships to land so that passengers could walk to the shore.

Eventually, they became popular as places to promenade and take the sea air for a small fee. Later, tea-rooms, theatres and amusements were added. Many piers fell into disuse and were eventually destroyed. However you can see fine examples of Victorian piers at Brighton, Llandudno and Blackpool. There are about 55 Victorian piers still surviving in England and Wales for you to discover.

↓ The West Pier in Brighton was open to the public from 1872 to 1975. It burned down in 2003.

On the West Pier, Brighton.

At the beginning of the Victorian age most people lived in the countryside. Many of the towns and cities where we live today grew during Victoria's reign.

City living

People moved to where industry was situated and this was why the towns developed. In most industrial areas terraced houses were built for the workers. Shops, schools, churches, public houses and other businesses grew up around these areas. Many parts of our towns and cities have Victorian buildings that are still in use. You can track down these buildings in your local area. To get a taste of what it was like to live in Victorian times you can visit a living museum. Many of these museums re-create the Victorian era by re-erecting Victorian buildings and setting them up to look like they did in Victorian times.

At the Black Country Living Museum, Victorian omnibuses and trams help to make the streets feel real. At Beamish in County Durham, actors dressed in Victorian clothes play the parts of shopkeepers and workers. This helps visitors to feel like they have stepped back in time.

↓ Weighing out sweets in the shop at Beamish, a living museum in County Durham.

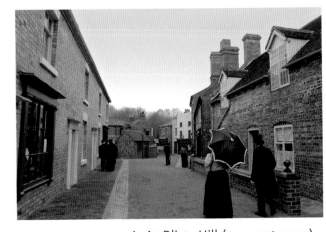

▲ At Blists Hill (see next page) you can experience what streets were like before the motor car.

⬆ The printer's shop at Beamish.

Blists Hill Victorian Town

Another living museum which aims to recreate Victorian times is Blists Hill Victorian Town at the Ironbridge Gorge Museum near Telford. The experience begins with a visit to the bank where modern cash can be exchanged for Victorian money. You can use the old money in the many traditional shops that have been set up. At the bakers you can buy freshly-made bread and at the druggist there are traditional remedies for sale. Blists Hill also has ordinary homes, a working fairground, a school, a doctor's surgery and a public house.

GO VISIT

Victorian Workhouses

Many poor, ill, disabled or unemployed Victorians struggled to survive. As a last resort they applied to stay in workhouses. Men and women were separated and slept in different wards. Everyone was expected to work. You can get an idea of how grim it was to live in a workhouse by visiting the Workhouse Museum at Ripon, Yorkshire or Southwell Workhouse, Nottinghamshire.

GRAND HOMES FOR THE RICH

Wealthy industrialists and manufacturers built many grand houses. Some of these have stood the test of time and you can track them down in your local area.

Town houses

Home life was important to the Victorians. However, only the rich could afford to build their own homes. In the towns and cities, the grand town houses had many storeys. The kitchen was in the basement, the dining room was on the ground floor and the drawing room was on the first floor. Above this were the adults' rooms, then the nursery and children's bedrooms. The rooms in the attic were for the servants. Many of these large town houses have since been divided into flats.

↑ Embroideries with the saying 'Home, Sweet Home' hung on the walls of both rich and poor houses.

GO VISIT

Abbey-Cwm-Hir Hall, Powys, Wales

The Hall at Abbey-Cwm-Hir in rural mid-Wales is a fine example of Victorian architecture. The 52-room house was started in 1833 and is one of the best surviving Victorian houses in Wales. Visitors can see all the rooms, including the snooker room with its stained glass ceiling and the domestic quarters with its collection of kitchen equipment. At Christmas, each room is decorated in Victorian festive style.

← The impressive snooker room at Abbey-Cwm-Hir was added in 1894.

Country homes

In the countryside there was more space to build magnificent stately homes with huge gardens. Some of these houses had large public rooms, such as halls and ballrooms, for entertaining. There were also private rooms just for the family. These houses needed armies of servants to run the household and look after the family.

➜ A grand bedroom – the Owl Suite – at Cragside.

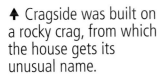

▲ Cragside was built on a rocky crag, from which the house gets its unusual name.

'The palace of a modern magician'

One of the most extraordinary Victorian houses that you can visit today is Cragside in Northumberland. The former home of wealthy industrialist Lord William George Armstrong, Cragside was the first house in the world to be lit by hydroelectricity. In the grounds you can see the artificial lakes, generators and pump houses that Armstrong had built to provide power for the house. The Victorians tried to invent many labour-saving devices and Armstrong was no exception. In his house you can see some of his curious inventions, such as the electric-powered cooking spit. In his greenhouse you will find the plant-pot turning machine used to ripen the peaches on all sides.

CHILDREN AND SCHOOLS

Life was not easy for rich or poor children. Poor children were expected to work from an early age, and rich children had to follow strict rules.

Victorian childhood

In the countryside, many poorer children helped on farms; in towns they worked in the factories. At the beginning of the age there were few laws to protect these children and many did dangerous jobs and worked long hours. Children from better-off families did not face the same hardships but they were expected to obey their parents and spend many hours studying the Bible.

▼ Many children lived in poverty in Victorian times, and couldn't afford to go to school. However things began to improve after the Education Act of 1881.

School days

There was no school system at the beginning of the Victorian era. Poor children sometimes attended Sunday school run by the Church of England. By 1839, these Church schools received some

funding from government and were set up as weekly elementary schools. One teacher looked after all the pupils and trained the older pupils to teach the younger children. Later, Ragged Schools were set up to teach homeless street children. In 1881, it became law that all children should attend elementary school. Many poor parents did not like their children going to school because they needed them to work. Often rich children had a governess or tutor who taught them at home. Boys were usually sent away to private secondary schools.

GO VISIT

Great Cressingham Victorian School

You can experience what it was like to go to elementary school in Victorian times at the Great Cressingham Victorian School in Norfolk. The school was originally opened in 1840. It is now a living museum and runs classes for seven-to-twelve-year olds as if it were 1898. Each child has a slate and a dip pen. The teacher stands at the front of the classroom while children sit at rows of desks. The children learn by repeating the same things over and over. At playtime they go outside and play with typical Victorian toys such as spinning tops, metal hoops and skittles.

▲ Inside the classroom at Great Cressingham Victorian School. Visiting children even dress in Victorian costume.

Punishments

Punishments for breaking school rules were often harsh. The cane was used on hands and backs. Children were given a stroke or 'cut' of the cane for being late, talking in class, answering back, failure to do homework or even kissing another pupil. You may be able to find out more about punishments at school by tracking down a punishment book. Every school kept one and you may find one in a local museum. In addition to caning pupils, slow learners were punished by being made to stand at the back of the class wearing a dunce's cap, a tall hat with a 'D' on it.

VICTORIAN HEALTH

Death and disease touched the lives of all Victorians, whether they were rich or poor.

➜ A scene from the slums of London in the 1870s.

Death and disease

Diseases such as cholera, consumption, typhoid and diphtheria killed millions of people. In the early years of Victoria's reign half of all children living in the towns died before their fifth birthday. In parts of London the life expectancy of a well-off person was 45 years, compared to 22 years for a labourer. Part of the problem was that nobody understood how diseases spread until the end of the 19th century. They did not realise the importance of hygiene. The death rate amongst the poor was higher because they lived in overcrowded, dirty slums. Only the rich could afford to pay a doctor or buy medicine.

Early surgery

In the early days of Queen Victoria's reign, people were suspicious of surgeons. The work they did involved slicing flesh and cutting off limbs. Surgeons also learned about anatomy by cutting up dead bodies, some of which were stolen from graveyards. By comparison the doctor or physician was a gentleman who kept his hands clean. Patients visited him at his surgery or he visited them at home. Patients had to pay the doctor so illness was greatly feared by the poor.

▲ Inside the Old Operating Theatre in London.

GO VISIT

Gladstone Pottery Museum, Stoke-on-Trent

Some doctors set up surgeries in working-class areas. You can visit the doctor's house at Gladstone Pottery Museum in Stoke-on-Trent. It represents the home and surgery of a doctor in the 1880s. The doctor here would have seen many workers with chest problems from breathing in dust and lead from the pottery glazes.

➜ Inside the doctor's surgery at the Gladstone Pottery Museum. It is set up as it might have been in the 1890s.

The Old Operating Theatre

Despite people's fears, operations were sometimes necessary. The operating theatre was opened in 1822 in the attic of St Thomas's Church, London. In those days surgery was done without anaesthetics and antiseptic. Patients had to be held down while the surgeon did his job. Today you can see the actual operating table where these operations took place. By the 1850s, ether and chloroform were being used as anaesthetic. This allowed surgeons more time to operate and less people died. In 1867, Joseph Lister discovered antiseptic which helped to reduce the risk of infection.

CRIME AND PUNISHMENT

Crime was a huge problem in Victorian times. The Victorians dealt with the situation by passing laws about punishment and reforming the prisons. They also set up the first police forces.

'Bobbies' on 'the beat'

The middle-classes became richer with more possessions in Victorian times. At the same time the poor struggled to survive. The divide between rich and poor contributed to rising levels of crime. In 1829, the British home secretary, Sir Robert Peel, set up the first metropolitan police force in the country at Scotland Yard in London. These first policemen were nicknamed 'bobbies' or 'peelers' after Sir Robert Peel. Each constable worked a 14-hour shift on which they walked a regular route called 'the beat'. The police were so successful in London that similar forces were set up elsewhere. In 1862, it became law that every town in the country should have its own force.

↓ Victorian police constables were issued with blue uniforms and top hats.

▲ Victorian punishments were harsh, to deter people from committing crimes again. This picture shows young prisoners at Tothill Fields prison in 1861.

Galleries of Justice

At the National Centre for Citizenship and Law: Galleries of Justice in Nottingham's Lace Market you can step back in time and find out more about the history of the police force and law and order in Britain. The Nottinghamshire police force was started in 1840 but the Galleries of Justice was a court and prison from the 1780s to the 1980s. Today, visitors can experience what it was like to be arrested, placed in the dock of a Victorian courtroom and sentenced to death, transportation or jail. They can then take a look around actual cells and wonder how people slept eight to a double bed and made do without any toilets. The museum also has the HM Prison Service collection, which includes the largest collection of hand-cuffs and leg-irons in Britain.

GO VISIT

Judges Lodgings, Presteigne, Wales

The Judges Lodgings at Presteigne in Wales is a good place to find out what a real courthouse was like in the 1870s. Visitors can also tour the judge's private accommodation which includes the drawing room, dining room, bathroom and bedroom set up as it was in Victorian times. Of special interest is the dark, damp cells where prisoners were kept (below).

GLOSSARY

Anaesthetics Drugs used to make someone unable to feel pain.

Antiseptic Substance used to kill germs.

Chloroform An anaesthetic – see above.

Cholera A serious disease that causes vomiting and diarrhoea.

Church of England The established Protestant religion, of which Queen Victoria was the head.

Constitutional monarchy Where the monarch (the king or queen) is the Head of State but Parliament runs the country. The UK is an example of a constitutional monarchy.

Consumption The Victorian name for the wasting disease, tuberculosis.

Dip pen A type of inkpen without an ink cartridge. The writer had to dip the pen into a small inkwell.

Diphtheria A serious disease that causes difficulty with breathing.

Druggist Someone who sells medicines.

Elementary schools The Victorian word for primary schools. Children left at the age of 12, usually to go to work.

Ether An anaesthetic drug, see above.

Generator A machine that generates power.

Gothic When referring to buildings, a style of building that uses many pointed arches and columns.

Home secretary An important government minister concerned with law and order.

Hull The part of a boat that lies under the water.

Hydroelectricity Electricity produced by water power.

Industrial Revolution The period in history when many changes came about due to the invention of machines.

Industrialists People who own factories, mills and other parts of industry.

Leg-irons Pieces of metal that went round each foot and were joined by a chain.

Life expectancy The number of years that someone might be expected to live.

Omnibus Victorian name for a bus.

Parliament The group of people that govern a country and make its laws.

Promenade To take a walk along a pier or a seafront.

Ragged Schools Free schools for poor children set up in Victorian times.

Screw propeller A propeller with several angled blades. As it rotates, the blades push against the water and propel a ship along.

Slate A piece of slate used by schoolchildren to write on with chalk.

Slum Very poor quality housing.

Steam locomotive The steam engine that pulled a train.

Traditional remedy Herbal or other medicine, rather than medicine from a chemist.

Tram A type of train that ran along rails through Victorian towns and cities.

Transportation The practice of sending criminals abroad – for example to Australia – to serve their sentences.

Typhoid A serious disease spread by dirty water and poor hygiene.

Viaduct A long bridge carrying a road or railway across a valley.

Workhouse The grim place where really poor people could go for shelter and food.

PLACES TO VISIT

Abbey-Cwm-Hir Hall
Abbey-Cwm-Hir
nr. Llandrindod Wells
Powys, LD1 6PH
www.abbeycwmhir.com

Balmoral Castle
Ballater
Aberdeenshire, AB35 5TB
www.balmoralcastle.com/

Beamish
County Durham, DH9 0RG
www.beamish.org.uk/

Black Country Living Museum
Tipton Road
Dudley, DY1 4SQ
www.bclm.co.uk/

Blackburn Museum and Art Gallery
Museum Street
Blackburn, BB1 7AJ
www.blackburn.gov.uk/museums

Blackpool Tower
The Promenade
Blackpool, FY1 4BJ
www.theblackpooltower.co.uk/

Blists Hill Victorian Town
Legges Way
Madeley, Ironbridge, TF7 5DU
*www.ironbridge.org.uk/our_attractions/
blists_hill_victorian_town/*

Buckingham Palace
Buckingham Palace Road
London, SW1A 1AA
*www.royal.gov.uk/TheRoyalResidences/
BuckinghamPalace/
BuckinghamPalace.aspx*

Clifton Suspension Bridge
Suspension Bridge Road
Clifton, Bristol, BS8 3PA
www.cliftonbridge.org.uk/

Cragside
Rothbury
Morpeth, NE65 7PX
www.nationaltrust.org.uk/cragside/

Galleries of Justice Museum
The Lace Market
Nottingham, NG1 1HN
www.galleriesofjustice.org.uk/

Gladstone Pottery Museum
Uttoxeter Road
Longton, Stoke-on-Trent, ST3 1PQ
www.stokemuseums.org.uk/gpm

Great Cressingham Victorian School
The Street
Great Cressingham, IP25 6NL
www.victorianschool.com/

Houses of Parliament
St Margaret Street
London, SW1A 2AT
www.parliament.uk/

Judges Lodgings Museum
Broad Street
Presteigne, Powys, LD8 2AD
www.judgeslodging.org.uk/

National Railway Museum
Leeman Road
York, YO26 4XJ
www.nrm.org.uk/

Old Operating Theatre
9a St. Thomas's St
London, SE1 9RY
www.thegarret.org.uk/

Osborne House
East Cowes,
Isle of Wight, PO32 6JY
*www.tourist-information-uk.com/osborne-
house.htm*

Queen Street Mill Textile Museum
Harle Syke
Burnley, BB10 2HX
*www.lancashire.gov.uk/acs/sites/museums/
index.asp*

Ragged School Museum
46-50 Copperfield Rd
London, E3 4RR
www.raggedschoolmuseum.org.uk/

Royal Pavilion
Brighton, BN1 1EE
*www.brighton-hove-
rpml.org.uk/royalpavilion/aboutthepalace/
pages/home.aspx*

SS *Great Britain*
Great Western Dockyard
Bristol, BS1 6TY
www.ssgreatbritain.org/

Verdant Works
West Henderson's Wynd
Dundee, DD1 5BT
*www.rrdiscovery.com/
index.php?pageID=130*

Windsor Castle
Windsor
Berkshire, SL4 1NJ
*www.royalcollection.org.uk/visit/
windsorcastle*

Workhouse Museum
Allhallowgate
Ripon, HG4 1LE
*http://riponmuseums.co.uk/museums/
workhouse_museum_gardens*

WEBLINKS
www.bbc.co.uk/schools/primaryhistory/victorian_britain/
BBC website focusing on Victorian children. Packed with facts, photos, video clips and activities.

www.spartacus.schoolnet.co.uk/PRvictoria.htm
Website about Queen Victoria, with many links to other important people and events.

www.victorians.org.uk/
Virtual Victorians website where you can follow the daily lives of two Victorian factory workers.

Note to parents and teachers
Every effort has been made by the Publishers to ensure that the websites in this book are suitable for children, that they are of the highest educational value, and that they contain no inappropriate or offensive material. However, because of the nature of the Internet, it is impossible to guarantee that the contents of these sites will not be altered. We strongly advise that Internet access is supervised by a responsible adult.

INDEX